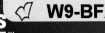
CORNERSTONES OF FREEDOM™

The INDUSTRIAL REVOLUTION

BY MELISSA McDANIEL

CHILDREN'S PRESS®

An Imprint of Scholastic Inc.
New York Toronto London Auckland Sydney
Mexico City New Delhi Hong Kong
Danbury, Connecticut

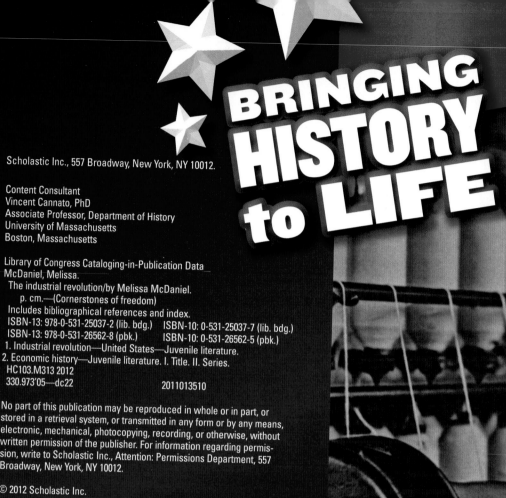

BRINGING HISTORY to LIFE

Scholastic Inc., 557 Broadway, New York, NY 10012.

Content Consultant
Vincent Cannato, PhD
Associate Professor, Department of History
University of Massachusetts
Boston, Massachusetts

Library of Congress Cataloging-in-Publication Data
McDaniel, Melissa.
  The industrial revolution/by Melissa McDaniel.
    p. cm.—(Cornerstones of freedom)
  Includes bibliographical references and index.
  ISBN-13: 978-0-531-25037-2 (lib. bdg.)   ISBN-10: 0-531-25037-7 (lib. bdg.)
  ISBN-13: 978-0-531-26562-8 (pbk.)   ISBN-10: 0-531-26562-5 (pbk.)
  1. Industrial revolution—United States—Juvenile literature.
  2. Economic history—Juvenile literature. I. Title. II. Series.
  HC103.M313 2012
  330.973'05—dc22   2011013510

8 9 10 R 21 20 19 18 17

Photographs © 2012: age fotostock/Florian Monheim: 8; Alamy Images:
46 (Classic Image), 12 (William Robinson Derbyshire); Getty Images: 38
(Fotosearch), 4 top, 24 (JupiterImages), 36 (SSPL); iStockphoto/Steve
Geer: 14; Library of Congress: cover (Lewis Wickes Hine), 57 (George
McCormick), 37 (Charles Wilson Peale), 13, 56 top (Wright/Posselwhite),
18; Melissa McDaniel: 64; NEWSCOM: 30 bottom (akg-images), 15 (Samuel
Smiles/KPA/United Archives/WHA); North Wind Picture Archives: 21
(Nancy Carter), 10, 11, 16, 20, 26, 27, 28, 34, 35, 56 bottom, 59 top; Photo
Researchers, NY: 2, 3, 48 (Lewis Hine), 40 (Winslow Homer/Omikron),
4 bottom, 30 top, 31, 47 (Omikron), 17 (Science, Industry and Business
Library/New York Public Library), 5 bottom, 54 (Inga Spence), 45 (SPL), 22;
Redux Pictures/Jim West/Report Digital-REA: back cover; Superstock,
Inc.: 25 (age fotostock), 51 (Everett Collection), 49 (Robert Harding Picture
Library), 7, 42 (Image Asset Management Ltd.), 44 (Universal Images
Group); The Granger Collection, New York: 5 top, 32, 43, 59 bottom;
University of Massachusetts Lowell: 50.

Did you know that studying history can be fun?

BRING HISTORY TO LIFE by becoming a history investigator. Examine the evidence (primary and secondary source materials); cross-examine the people and witnesses. Take a look at what was happening at the time—but be careful! What happened years ago might suddenly become incredibly interesting and change the way you think!

Contents

A Need for Machines

How is a shirt made? Before the mid-1700s, it was a time-consuming, eye-straining, finger-aching process. First, a person had to get some cotton that had already been cleaned and combed. The cotton fibers then had to be spun into yarn. Someone sat working a spinning wheel, which was used to twist the fibers together to make one long piece of yarn. The yarn might then be dyed to give it color. Then it was woven into cloth on a **loom**. A pattern for the shirt was placed on the cloth. The cloth was cut and carefully stitched together by hand. At last, the shirt was completed.

Cotton clothes were actually rare at this time. Cotton fibers twist naturally, making them hard to work with. Most clothes were made of wool, which was spun and woven in the same long process.

Some people spun their own yarn and wove their own fabric. Other people bought fabric, but it was expensive. People sometimes worked in their own homes, making yarn, fabric, or clothing for sale. But

THE EARLIEST LOOMS DATE

one person working with simple tools could not produce much.

In Great Britain in the mid-1700s, ideas were brewing that would change the way people worked. People began inventing machines to do the work better and faster than people could. Then inventors came up with better ways to power the machines. The **textile** industry moved out of the home and into the factory. It was the beginning of the Industrial Revolution.

Making clothing by hand is a long, difficult process.

CHAPTER 1

INTO THE FACTORY

Cromford Mill in Great Britain was one of the earliest industrial factories.

SIR RICHARD ARKWRIGHT & CO.

ESTABLISHED 1769

IN 1771, A LARGE BRICK building five stories high was erected along the River Derwent in Derbyshire, in the Midlands of England. It was called Cromford Mill. Each day, 200 workers trudged through the front gate just before 6 a.m. Many were children, some as young as seven years old. Many of the workers were women. They spent 12 hours tending machines that spun cotton into yarn. As they left at 6 p.m., 200 more women and children passed through the gate to work the night shift.

Cromford Mill was the first cotton-spinning mill built by Richard Arkwright, one of the driving forces behind the Industrial Revolution. It made him a very rich man.

Many looms were large, complicated devices.

Small Steps

The Industrial Revolution was not the result of a single inventor or a single invention. In the middle of the 1700s, many inventors were working on solving the same problems. One of their main concerns was speeding up the process of making yarn and cloth.

On a traditional loom, all weaving was done by hand. The weaver held a **shuttle** that contained yarn, passing it over and under the rows of yarn held by the loom. In 1733, John Kay invented an instrument called the flying shuttle. The weaver did not have to hold the flying shuttle. Instead, the flying shuttle was attached to the loom, and the weaver controlled it with a lever. The flying shuttle sped up the weaving process and allowed weavers to make cloth that was wider than the length of their arms.

The next major improvement in the textile industry took place in 1764, when James Hargreaves developed the spinning jenny. This machine allowed workers to spin cotton into thread much more quickly.

The spinning jenny made it easier to make large amounts of thread.

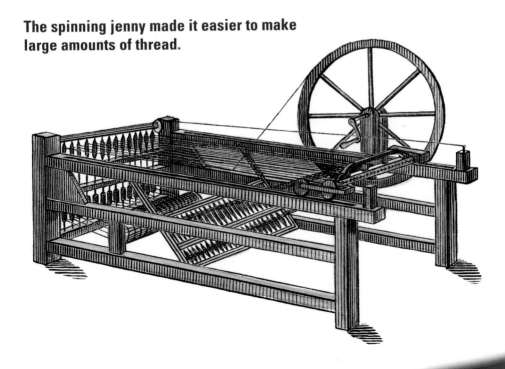

Arkwright used water to power the machines at Cromford Mill.

Around the same time, Richard Arkwright developed the spinning frame. It, too, increased the amount of thread that could be spun by a single person. At first, Arkwright used horses to run his spinning frame. He soon realized that a waterwheel would be a better way to power the machine. All that was needed was a rushing river. The moving water would do the work, and it never got tired or needed to be fed.

Arkwright changed the name of his machine to the "water frame" and soon built Cromford Mill.

Mills soon sprung up across England. There were so many textile mills in Manchester that it became known as Cottonopolis. By 1785, 16 million pounds (7 million kilograms) of cotton were being spun into thread every year in Great Britain. This was more than 30 times the amount that had been produced just 20 years earlier.

Using Steam

In the 1700s, other people focused on trying to find a way to use steam to power machines. Thomas Newcomen developed the first successful steam power plant in 1712.

Then, in 1765, James Watt designed a steam engine that

SPOTLIGHT ON

Richard Arkwright

Richard Arkwright was the youngest of 13 children born to a poor family in Lancashire, England. He became a wigmaker and invented a waterproof dye for the wigs. He used the money he earned from his invention to improve cotton-spinning machines. With the help of partners, Arkwright developed several different machines. They included a carding machine, which pulled cotton into long fibers, and the water frame, which spun cotton into yarn. But perhaps his most important accomplishment was establishing cotton-spinning mills. By combining power, machinery, and workers, he created the modern factory system.

This building in Dudley, in west central England, once housed an early steam engine.

was a great improvement on Newcomen's design. It used much less fuel, so it was much cheaper to run. With Watt's steam engine, cotton mills no longer had to be located next to rivers. They could be established anywhere.

The steam engine was also able to power many other types of machines in other industries. Flour mills run

A FIRSTHAND LOOK AT
A JAMES WATT STEAM ENGINE

James Watt's work on the steam engine helped power the Industrial Revolution. Throughout the 1790s, he continued to improve his steam engines. He made them more efficient. He also made some that were small, so they could be used in smaller workshops and not just in large factories. See page 60 for a link to view an original drawing of one of Watt's steam engines.

by steam engines could be moved away from rivers and located close to wheat fields. Steam engines were used to pump water out of mines. They also were used in the manufacture of iron. The steam engine allowed industry to grow in regions throughout England.

Steam engines provided power to a variety of different machines.

Growth and Change

The steam engine helped Great Britain grow and prosper, but it also made the country a dirtier place. Coal was burned to heat the water that became steam. Burning coal sent massive amounts of black smoke into the air. The smoke hung in the air, blotting out the sunlight.

The beginning of the Industrial Revolution changed England in other ways, too. Many people left their homes in the countryside and moved to the towns and cities where the mills were located. Many factory owners, including Richard Arkwright, built housing for workers next to the mills.

Early factories released huge amounts of black smoke.

Factory work was very different from the jobs most people had before the Industrial Revolution.

Working in the growing cities was very different from working in the countryside. People in cities generally did not work outdoors. They could not work at their own pace as they had when they were spinning thread at home. Instead, they labored inside large, loud factories. The machines set the pace. Many people earned a better living than they had in the countryside, but they sacrificed a bit of their independence for this higher salary.

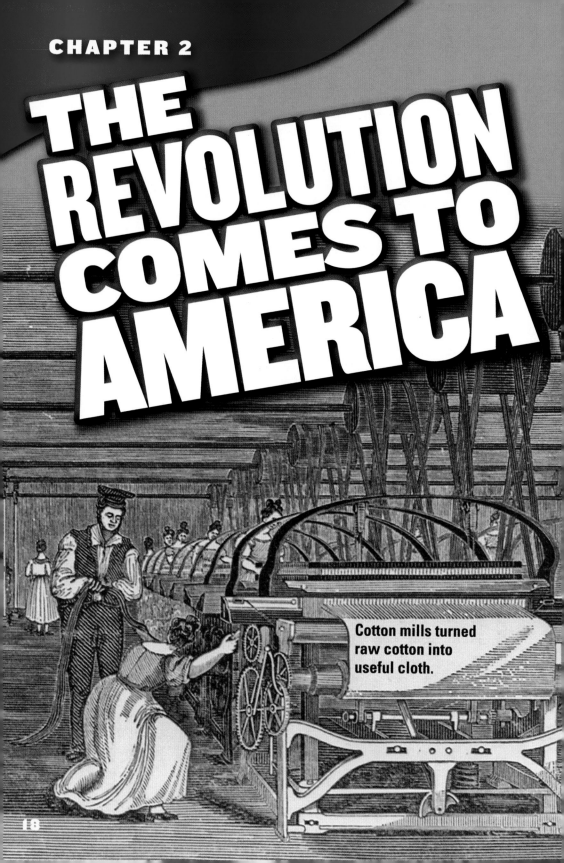

CHAPTER 2

THE REVOLUTION COMES TO AMERICA

Cotton mills turned raw cotton into useful cloth.

IN 1789, 21-YEAR-OLD Samuel Slater arrived in London to buy a boat ticket to America. He claimed to be a farmer, but this was not true. At the time, British law did not allow textile workers to leave the country, and Slater had worked at a cotton mill for years.

British law also banned anyone from sharing technological information with people from other countries. But Slater had a fantastic memory. He had memorized every detail of the machinery at Cromford Mill, including the workings of Richard Arkwright's water frame.

At the time, Britain was far more technologically advanced than the United States. Slater dreamed of making a fortune bringing these British **innovations** to America. With everything he needed stored safely in his memory, Slater sailed for New York.

Samuel Slater changed the U.S. economy by bringing his knowledge of British factories to America.

The First Factory

When he arrived in America, Slater offered his services and his knowledge to a man named Moses Brown, who wanted to build a water-powered cotton-spinning mill. "If I do not make yarn as good as they do in England, I will have nothing for my services," Slater told Brown.

By 1793, Slater and Brown had built a completely water-powered cotton-spinning mill next to the Blackstone River in Pawtucket, Rhode Island. Slater Mill

Slater Mill was used solely to produce cotton thread until 1829. After that, different companies produced other goods there.

was the first true factory in the United States. For this accomplishment, Slater is known as the Father of the American Industrial Revolution.

King Cotton

Mills soon popped up next to many of New England's rushing streams. Cotton fibers were spun into thread at these mills much more quickly than before. America's

Eli Whitney's cotton gin enabled cotton production to increase greatly in the American South.

cloth industry, however, was not quite ready to blossom because cotton was very expensive.

Cotton grows well in the southern United States. But the fluffy balls of cotton that grow on plants are peppered with tiny black seeds. In the early 1790s, the only way to remove the seeds was to pick them out by hand. It took a worker an entire day to remove the seeds from a single pound (0.5 kg) of cotton.

A man named Eli Whitney would solve this problem. Whitney, a native of Massachusetts, was working in

A FIRSTHAND LOOK AT
ELI WHITNEY'S COTTON GIN

Eli Whitney's cotton gin used rotating brushes spiked with sharp metal teeth to separate seeds from cotton. The teeth grabbed the cotton fibers and pulled them through a grid, leaving the seeds behind. Whitney **patented** his cotton gin in 1794. Receiving the patent from the U.S. government gave him the legal rights to make and sell his invention. See page 60 for links to view a model of Whitney's cotton gin, the original documents he submitted to the government for a patent, and an original drawing of the machine he sent with the patent papers.

Georgia in 1792. He heard about the problem cotton growers had and began working on a solution. By the following year, he had designed a method to separate the seeds from the cotton. He called his invention the cotton gin (*gin* is short for *engine*). Using the cotton gin, one person could now clean 50 pounds (23 kg) of cotton in a day.

The cotton gin transformed the economy of the American South. In 1793, about 5 million pounds (2 million kg) of cotton was grown in the United States. Ten years later, the nation was producing about 40 million pounds (18 million kg) of cotton each year. Cotton production continued to surge in the following decades. Cotton had become king of the southern economy. Cotton mills in New England and Europe could not get enough of it.

SPOTLIGHT ON

Slavery and the Cotton Gin

Southern cotton growers relied on slave labor to pick and process their cotton. The introduction of the cotton gin allowed production to soar, but planters needed more people to pick the cotton. More enslaved Africans were brought to America for this purpose. In 1790, there were about 700,000 slaves in the nation. By 1810, the total had grown to 1.2 million. In the decades that followed, cotton began to be grown in American lands farther west. The institution of slavery followed. Between 1810 and 1860, about 500,000 enslaved people were forced west to pick cotton. Some were sent as far west as Texas.

The Waltham System

Slater's Mill had been the very beginning of industrialization in the United States. Great Britain still had far superior textile mills. In 1810, a prominent Boston businessman named Francis Cabot Lowell traveled to England. During the two years he lived there, he toured many textile mills in England and Scotland. Like Slater before him, Lowell had an excellent memory. He carefully studied the machinery in the mills. In 1812 he returned home having fully memorized the workings of a power loom.

Using this knowledge, Lowell built a mill in Waltham, Massachusetts, just outside Boston, in 1814. The building housed the entire cotton manufacturing

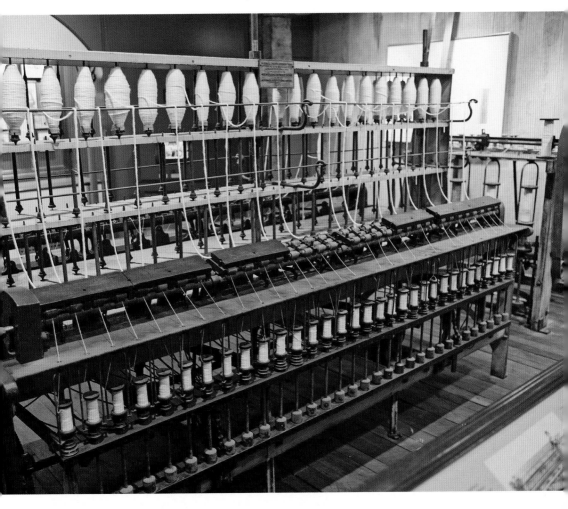

Cotton mills were made up of many machines.

process. Raw cotton was brought into the building.
There it was spun, dyed, and woven into finished cloth.
Putting all the steps under a single roof was a faster and
less expensive process than moving the cotton from mill
to mill for each step. This efficient method of production
was known first as the Waltham system and later as the
Lowell system.

The cotton industry provided new opportunities for young women in New England.

The power loom and other machines in Lowell's mills were larger than those in cotton-spinning mills like Slater's. Because of this, Lowell could not hire children as Slater did. Instead, he hired young single women as textile workers. They were called Lowell Girls. Most of his employees were ages 15 to 25. He built boardinghouses for them to live in and provided them with educational opportunities.

In the years between 1830 and 1860, the women earned $3.00 to $3.50 a week. This was generally a higher wage than they could find elsewhere, especially in the countryside. Much of the money they earned went to male family members to further their educations.

Larger cities began to develop in New England as industry and populations boomed.

SPOTLIGHT ON

Immigrant Labor

The machines and new technology used in most early factories allowed the work to be done by unskilled laborers. These were people who could be quickly taught how to do a specific job and then do it repeatedly. Skilled workers—such as doctors, lawyers, artisans, and craftspeople—required specialized training to do their work.

The huge number of immigrants coming to America beginning in the mid-1800s provided factories with an endless flow of unskilled labor. The hard work performed by immigrants contributed to the spread of factories and to the development and growth of large cities throughout the United States.

CHAPTER 3

ON THE MOVE

The United States expanded westward during the 1800s.

COTTON WAS GROWN IN THE
South and turned into fabric in the North. At
the beginning of the 1800s, cotton growers were
looking for new fields to cultivate farther west.
People in the North were also pushing west,
looking for new land and new opportunities.
Reaching these distant places was a difficult task.
Most roads between major cities were in ill repair,
filled with ruts and potholes. It took a week to
travel from New York to Boston. Today that trip can
be made in four hours. America needed to improve
its transportation network for industries in the
United States to continue to develop and fuel the
nation's growth.

The National Road

In 1802, the **federal** government decided to build a road from the East Coast to the Mississippi River. It would be called the National Road. Work began in 1811 in Cumberland, Maryland, and reached Wheeling, in what is now West Virginia, by 1818. Construction of the road

The National Road made travel easier for Americans moving westward.

Large rivers made excellent shipping routes, and they helped agriculture and cities expand inland.

then stopped for many years. Eventually, the National Road reached Vandalia, Illinois. But it never did make it all the way to the Mississippi.

The National Road was often crowded with wagons and stagecoaches, and it served as an important route for settlers moving west.

On the Water

Roads took a long time to build, and they were costly to maintain. It was also hard to move heavy goods over them. Waterways, on the other hand, were cheap and reliable. Being on a **navigable** waterway helped cities grow. New York was a huge shipping center because it connected the Atlantic Ocean and the Hudson River. Similarly, New Orleans was a leading shipping center in the South because it sat at the point where the Gulf of Mexico and the Mississippi River meet.

Yet there were not many large rivers that connected the Atlantic Ocean to regions farther inland. Waterways called canals were constructed to overcome this problem.

Getting goods from the East Coast to the Midwest was particularly difficult. The Midwest was home to the Great Lakes, but the lakes did not connect to large navigable rivers. DeWitt Clinton, a New York politician, began pushing for a canal that would connect Buffalo, on the shores of Lake Erie, with the Hudson River in Albany.

Connecting Lake Erie and the Hudson River would require building a canal 363 miles (584 kilometers) long. It was a huge project, but the Erie Canal was built in only eight years. After it opened in 1825, goods could be taken by boat from the Atlantic Ocean, up the Hudson River, across the Erie Canal, and into Lake

The Erie Canal made it easier to transport goods all around the country.

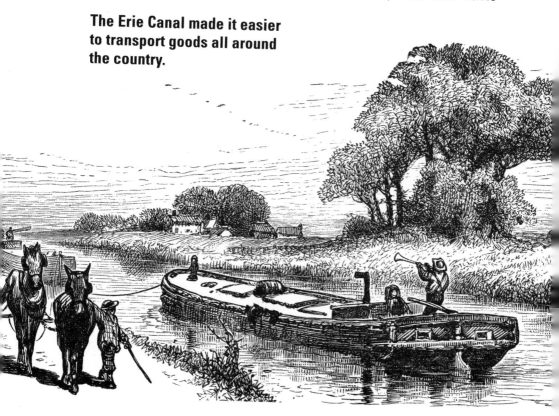

A FIRSTHAND LOOK AT
THE ERIE CANAL

Built between 1817 and 1825, the Erie Canal was the first transportation link connecting New York City to the Great Lakes. The canal provided transportation that was faster than animals pulling carts, and it reduced transport costs by an estimated 95 percent. Construction cost about $7 million at the time, roughly equal to $132 million today. When the idea was proposed to President Thomas Jefferson, he said the outrageous costs made the project "a little short of madness." See page 60 for a link to view an 1831 painting by John William Hill showing a part of the canal.

Erie. From there, goods could easily be transported throughout the Great Lakes region and the Midwest.

The canal became a busy highway. "In either direction, as far as the eye can see, long lines of boats can be observed. By night, their flickering head lamps give the impression of swarms of fireflies," reported one visitor.

The Erie Canal had a huge economic impact on the growing country. Timber, minerals, and crops were shipped out of the Midwest to the East. Farming tools, textiles, and other manufactured goods were shipped west, where families were starting farms. Before the canal opened, it took two weeks to ship wheat from Buffalo to New York City. Using the canal, it took less than four days and cost just one-twelfth of what it had before.

Cities along the Erie Canal and the Great Lakes boomed. Between 1830 and 1840, the population of Buffalo rose from about 8,600 to more than 18,000.

The Erie Canal also helped make New York City the most important East Coast port in the nation. The city experienced a huge burst of economic growth as goods flowed through the port, and countless travelers came to the city to establish businesses and homes. Soon, other canals crisscrossed the American landscape. By 1850, the nation boasted more than 3,700 miles (6,000 km) of canals.

New York City became one of the country's major ports.

Robert Fulton's steamboat was an impressive sight for its time.

The Power of Steam

In 1800, traveling by boat downriver was easy, but traveling against a river's current was not. How does a large boat loaded with tons of grain, ore, or machinery travel upstream? The answer was steam power. People had been experimenting with steamboats since the late 1700s. But it wasn't until 1807 that they became practical to use.

Steamboats made shipping much easier and faster.

On August 17, 1807, inventor Robert Fulton took the *North River Steamboat* 150 miles (240 km) up the Hudson River. Fulton's steamboat moved at an average speed of 4.5 miles per hour (7.2 kph). That's only about the rate of a brisk walk, but it was impressive at the time. Shipbuilders rushed to build steamboats. In the coming years, engines were improved, and the boats were able to travel faster. By 1855, there were 727 steamboats sailing the Mississippi and Ohio Rivers.

Laying Track

Soon, canal boats and steamboats would have a new competitor. It was the train. The Baltimore and Ohio Railroad was the first successful steam-powered railroad in the United States. In 1830, the company laid 13 miles (21 km) of track out from Baltimore.

In the coming years railroad tracks would be laid all across the nation. In 1840, 3,326 miles (5,353 km) of track crisscrossed the United States. By 1860, that number had increased to 30,600 miles (49,250 km). In 1869, the **Transcontinental** Railroad was completed. The East and West Coasts of the growing nation were now connected by railroad.

YESTERDAY'S HEADLINES

Robert Fulton's steamboat ride up the Hudson was an exciting moment. An article in the *American Citizen* on August 17, 1807, reported,

Mr. Fulton's ingenious Steam Boat, invented with a view to the navigation of the Mississippi from New Orleans upwards, sails today from the North River, . . . to Albany. The velosity [sic] of the Steam Boat is calculated at four miles an hour; it is said that it will make a progress of two against the current of the Mississippi; and if so it will certainly be a very valuable acquisition to the commerce of the Western States.

Railroads allowed companies to ship their goods to the western parts of the country.

Railroads had many advantages when compared to water travel. They could be used year-round because they didn't freeze in the winter. They could be built practically anywhere. Tracks were laid across deserts and through mountain passes. Bridges carried railroad tracks across rivers and over gorges.

Railroads were also very good at transporting large amounts of cargo from one place to another. Towns and cities flourished wherever track was laid. Towns that were farther away from the railroad withered. Farmers and ranchers could easily get their crops to market if a railroad was nearby. Railroads brought people in the countryside a little bit closer to the rest of the nation. As track was laid across the country, more and more settlers pushed farther west. They moved across prairies and through the deserts. The United States had become a continental nation.

A VIEW FROM ABROAD

In 1842, the English author Charles Dickens visited America and rode on a train. He later described his experiences, writing:

On it whirls headlong, dives through the woods again, emerges in the light, clatters over frail arches, rumbles upon the heavy ground, shoots beneath a wooden bridge which intercepts the light for a second like a wink, suddenly awakens all the slumbering echoes in the main street of a large town, . . . On, on, on tears the mad dragon of an engine with its train of cars; scattering in all directions a shower of burning sparks from its wood fire; screeching, hissing, yelling, panting.

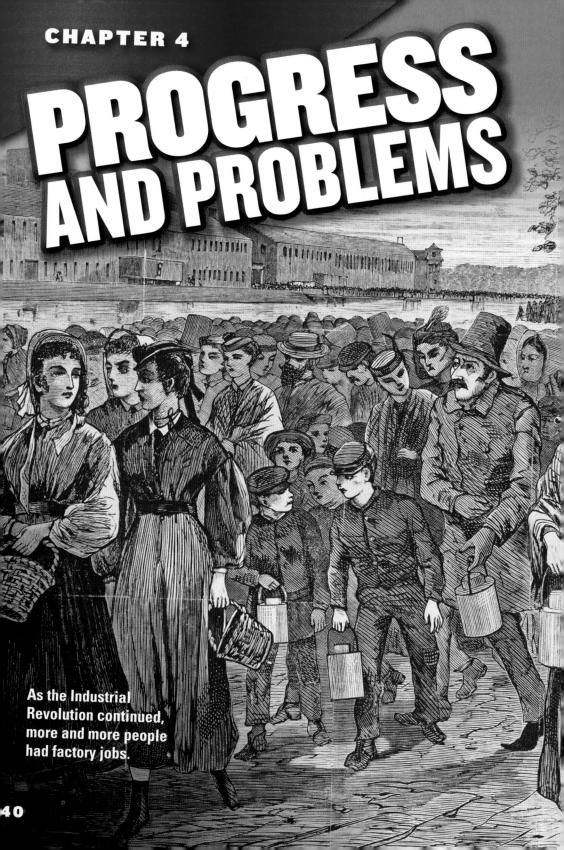

CHAPTER 4

PROGRESS AND PROBLEMS

As the Industrial Revolution continued, more and more people had factory jobs.

THE BOOM OF TECHNOLOGY

made 19th-century America an exciting, vibrant nation. Immigrants and people from the countryside poured into the cities to work in factories. New machines were being invented that increased production and made work more efficient. There were new metals to be made, new technologies to be uncovered. The Industrial Revolution was going full steam ahead.

The Industrial Revolution brought improved farming methods.

Changes on the Farm

Everyone was looking for better and faster ways to
do their jobs. During the mid-1800s, new machinery
changed farming. In 1831, Cyrus McCormick developed
a mechanical reaper, which **mechanized** the entire
harvesting process. No longer would farmers have to cut
wheat by hand. Using McCormick's mechanical reaper,
a farmer could harvest 8 acres (3.2 hectares) of wheat
in a day instead of 2 acres (0.8 ha). The reaper was so

revolutionary and strange, however, that farmers weren't even willing to try it. Not until the 1850s were thousands of reapers rumbling across the American fields.

Farmers adopted John Deere's steel plow much more quickly. Deere invented it in 1837. Using Deere's plow, farmers could sow, or plant, seeds much faster than they had before. **Threshing** machines were also developed, speeding up the harvest.

Dots and Dashes

Railroad tracks continued to be laid down at a furious pace as the century progressed. By 1920, more than 250,000 miles (400,000 km) of tracks crossed the

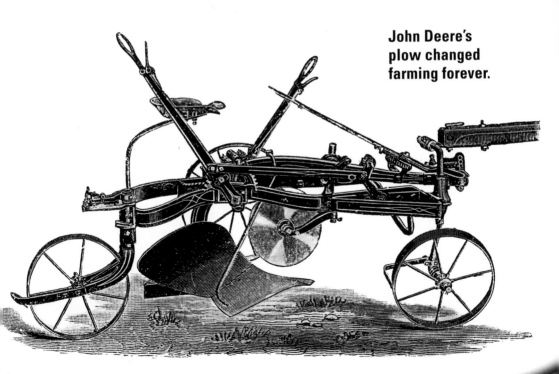

John Deere's plow changed farming forever.

The telegraph allowed for faster communication across long distances.

country. The railroad connected people who lived in distant corners of the nation. But there was also a need for a more immediate connection. People wanted to be able to communicate quickly over long distances.

In the 1830s and 1840s, Samuel F. B. Morse and Alfred Vail developed a way of sending messages over wires. A transmitter would send short or long bursts of electrical current—in the form of dots and dashes—over the wires. Morse and Vail created an alphabetic code using dots and dashes. Any word could be spelled out using them.

A FIRSTHAND LOOK AT
EARLY TELEGRAPH MESSAGES

The early telegraph system developed by Samuel Morse and Alfred Vail produced a paper copy on the receiving end of the message with raised dots and dashes. A telegraph operator translated the dots and dashes using the alphabetic code. On May 24, 1844, a telegraph line between Washington, D.C., and Baltimore, Maryland, was officially opened. The line connected the Supreme Court building to a railroad station in Baltimore. See page 60 for links to view the translation of the first official telegraph message ever sent, as well as other historic messages and a diagram of the original telegraph.

The first telegraph line was strung between Washington, D.C., and Baltimore, Maryland, in 1844. Telegraph wires were strung across the land. By 1866, more than 825,000 miles (1.3 million km) of telegraph wire crisscrossed the country.

Telegraphs were specialized machines that required expert operators.

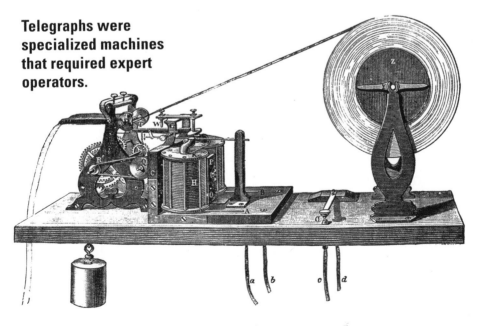

SPOTLIGHT ON

Working in a Factory

Factory work was often dangerous and dirty, and it was almost always boring and repetitive. After a visit to a paper factory in 1855, novelist Herman Melville wrote:

At rows of blank-looking counters sat rows of blank-looking girls, with blank, white folders in their blank hands, all blankly folding blank paper. Not a syllable was breathed. Nothing was heard but the low, steady, overruling hum of the iron animals. The human voice was banished from the spot.

The telegraph changed the speed of life. During the American Revolutionary War, the Battles of Lexington and Concord were fought on April 19, 1775. News of the battles didn't reach the Continental Congress in Philadelphia, Pennsylvania, until April 24. It was another month before the news reached London. With the telegraph, communication became instant.

Children at Work

Many children were put to work in factories from a very young age. In 1820, half of industrial workers in the United States were children, usually under the age of 10. Some children lost limbs in the dangerous machinery. The air inside the factories was often thick with **pollutants**. Many children became sick from breathing it. Many children who worked in factories did not have

Many children worked in factories and did not go to school until stricter labor laws were passed.

a chance to go to school. Their lives consisted of little beyond tending the factory machines and sleeping.

Slowly, some people began trying to change things. In 1836, Massachusetts passed the first state child labor law. It required all children under age 15 working in factories to attend school at least three months a year. In 1842, Massachusetts passed another law, which stated that children could work only 10 hours a day. Although other states soon passed child labor laws, they were seldom enforced.

Before child labor laws were enforced in the United States, children worked long hours in factories.

In the early 1900s, the federal government tried to enforce the state child labor laws, but their efforts failed. Finally, in 1938, the federal government began to regulate child labor. It banned children under 16 from working full-time in factories. Children 14 or 15 years old could only work during school vacations and outside of school hours.

Efforts to Improve Work Conditions

Many adults also objected to the long hours, low pay, and dangerous conditions in the factories. In 1834, women at the Lowell textile mills went on **strike** to protest a wage cut. After a few days, most of the women had returned to work at the lower wages. The strike had failed.

Two years later, the women went on strike again. This time it was to protest an increase in the rent they had to pay at the company's boardinghouses. One of the striking workers stood outside and gave a speech proclaiming how they had to resist the rent increase. This was considered shocking behavior. At the time, women typically did not give speeches in public.

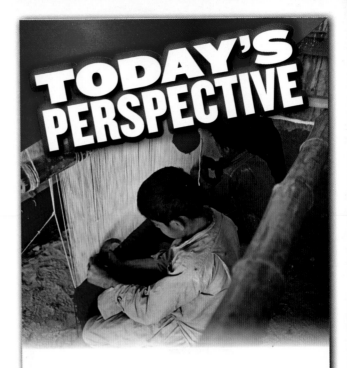

TODAY'S PERSPECTIVE

Today, children are no longer allowed to work in factories in the United States. But around the world, an estimated 250 million children ages 5 to 14 work. Nearly half work full-time, and many work in dangerous jobs. In 2008, an estimated 2.7 million Pakistani children between the ages of 10 and 14 had jobs. Many work in agriculture or on the street selling food or trinkets. Some, however, work in sweatshops. These are factories where people work long hours for little pay. In Pakistan and other countries, companies hire children because they can be paid less than adults.

Textile workers in Massachusetts, such as the ones in this picture, helped improve working conditions in neighboring New Hampshire.

About 2,500 workers walked off the job. Not enough workers remained to run all of the machinery. The strike continued for months. Eventually, the company agreed to eliminate the rent increase.

In the 1840s, many people who worked in mills in New England wanted to reduce the workday from 12 hours to 10 hours. They were not successful in Massachusetts at first. It was neighboring New Hampshire that became the first state to pass a law making the workday 10 hours long.

Industrial workers became used to standing up for themselves and making their beliefs known. Many began working to reform society on a larger scale. Some New England industrial workers, particularly women, became involved in the movement to end slavery. Others worked for women's rights. The Industrial Revolution had brought workers off farms and into mills. In their new environment, many workers began to speak up about the changing world.

Some industrial workers worked to secure greater rights for women, such as the right to vote.

What Happened Where?

America's transportation network Before the 1800s, most American cities were spread out along the East Coast. Getting from one to another was difficult. Going anywhere inland could take weeks. That changed in the early 1800s, as America's transportation network grew.

Promontory Summit

Transcontinental Railroad To build the Transcontinental Railroad, one group of workers started in the western United States and one started in the eastern United States. The two groups met at Promontory Summit, Utah, on May 10, 1869.

— Transcontinental Railroad, 1870
— Major railroads, 1870
— National Road, 1860
— Canals, 1860

MEXICO

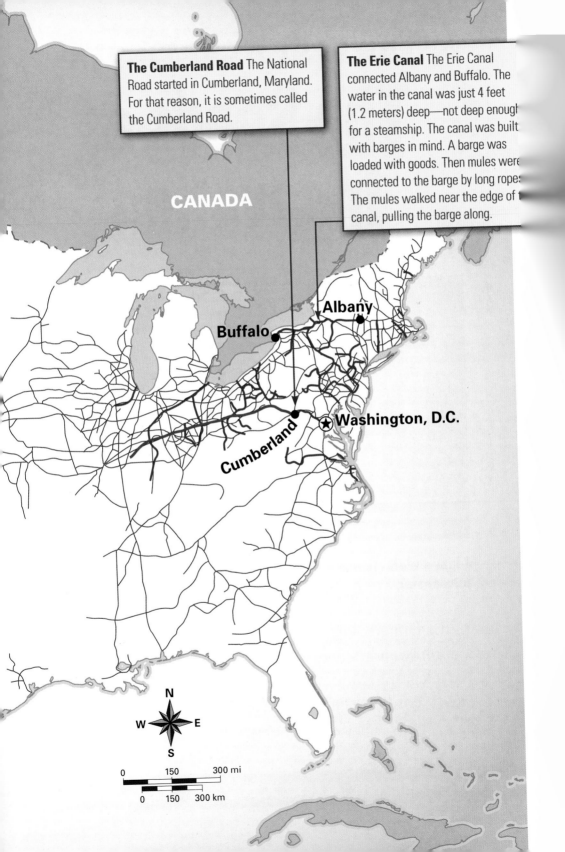

The Cumberland Road The National Road started in Cumberland, Maryland. For that reason, it is sometimes called the Cumberland Road.

The Erie Canal The Erie Canal connected Albany and Buffalo. The water in the canal was just 4 feet (1.2 meters) deep—not deep enough for a steamship. The canal was built with barges in mind. A barge was loaded with goods. Then mules were connected to the barge by long ropes. The mules walked near the edge of the canal, pulling the barge along.

CANADA

Albany

Buffalo

Cumberland

★ Washington, D.C.

N
W   E
S

0   150   300 mi

0   150   300 km

The Seeds of Innovation

Today's workers use a wide variety of technology to make their jobs easier.

As the United States entered the 20th century, industry and innovation kept booming. The telephone replaced the telegraph. Model T automobiles began rolling off Henry Ford's assembly line. By 1910, the United States was producing 187,000 cars per year.

In the 1920s, radio became an important tool for spreading information and entertaining the public. The homes of Americans became filled with **consumer** goods made in factories around the country. People bought refrigerators, bicycles, lawn mowers, electric lamps, and hundreds of other items to make life easier and more enjoyable.

Through it all, Americans continued to move to the cities and the suburbs. As farms became more mechanized, fewer workers were needed. The more the nation industrialized, the less rural it became.

The innovation that began with the Industrial Revolution continues to this day. In 1975, 20-year-old Bill Gates founded Microsoft, and computers soon became common in homes and offices everywhere. The later development of the Internet changed the way people all over the world lived and worked. Global communication had become immediate, in the form of e-mail, texting, and Internet chatting.

These developments and countless improvements in the fields of medicine, manufacturing, communication, and transportation were made possible by the seeds of innovation planted during the Industrial Revolution. Today, people look to the future with the same spirit of inventiveness and determination that the leaders of the Industrial Revolution displayed.

INFLUENTIAL INDIVIDUALS

Richard Arkwright

Richard Arkwright (1732–1792) helped develop the water frame, which spun cotton into yarn quickly. He also founded Cromford Mill, the first modern factory.

James Watt (1736–1819) was a Scottish inventor and engineer whose work on the steam engine helped start the Industrial Revolution in Great Britain.

Robert Fulton (1765–1815) was an inventor and engineer who built the first commercial steamboat.

Eli Whitney (1765–1825) was an inventor who developed the cotton gin, a machine for removing the seeds from cotton fibers. This development allowed the American cotton and textile industries to thrive.

Samuel Slater (1768–1835) brought his knowledge of English cotton-spinning technology to the United States and started a cotton mill in Rhode Island. For this, he is known as the Father of the American Industrial Revolution.

Samuel Slater

Francis Cabot Lowell (1775–1817) was a businessman who built America's first textile mill that turned raw cotton into finished cloth all in one building. The city of Lowell, Massachusetts, is named after him.

Samuel F. B. Morse (1791–1872) was one of the inventors of the telegraph, an instrument for sending long-distance messages.

John Deere (1804–1886) was a blacksmith who opened a shop in Grand Detour, Illinois, where he manufactured cast-steel plows, a vast improvement over the iron or wood plows farmers used at that time. His invention revolutionized farming and contributed to the growth of the Midwest in the 19th century.

Cyrus McCormick (1809–1884) invented a mechanical reaper to harvest grain. He founded the McCormick Harvesting Machine Company, which later became part of International Harvester.

Cyrus McCormick

Bill Gates (1955–) is a computer software developer who created Microsoft, a company that produces computer operating systems. The quality and affordability of the systems helped spur the computer boom of the late 20th century.

TIMELINE

1765
James Watt develops the steam engine.

1771
In Derbyshire, England, Richard Arkwright builds Cromford Mill, one of the first modern factories.

1793
Slater's Mill is built; Eli Whitney invents the cotton gin.

1807
Robert Fulton makes his first steamboat journey up the Hudson River.

1830
The Baltimore and Ohio, the first railroad in the United States, lays its first tracks.

1831
Cyrus McCormick invents the mechanical reaper.

1834
Female workers at the Lowell mills go on strike; it fails, but two years later, they do it again.

1836
Massachusetts passes the first state child labor law.

1811

Construction begins on the National Road.

1814

Francis Cabot Lowell builds a cotton mill in Waltham, Massachusetts.

1825

The Erie Canal opens.

1837

John Deere invents a steel plow.

1869

The Transcontinental Railroad is completed.

1938

The federal government passes a law limiting child labor.

LIVING HISTORY

Primary sources provide firsthand evidence about a topic. Witnesses to a historical event create primary sources. They include autobiographies, newspaper reports of the time, oral histories, photographs, and memoirs. A secondary source analyzes primary sources, and is one step or more removed from the event. Secondary sources include textbooks, encyclopedias, and commentaries.

Early Telegraph Messages To view a translation of the earliest message sent on the telegraph developed by Samuel Morse and Alfred Vail, as well as other historic messages and a diagram of the original telegraph, go to *http://international.loc.gov/ammem /sfbmhtml/sfbmhighlights01.html*

Eli Whitney's Cotton Gin and Patent Papers Eli Whitney's cotton gin made harvesting cotton faster and more efficient. To view a model of his device, go to *http://americanhistory.si.edu/collections /object.cfm?key=35&objkey=8981*

To see the documents Whitney submitted to the U.S. government for a patent and to view a 1794 illustration of the device, go to *www.archives.gov/education/lessons/cotton-gin-patent/#documents*

The Erie Canal Between 1829 and 1831, artist John William Hill painted several views of the recently completed Erie Canal. To view a watercolor painting of part of the canal near Little Falls, New York, go to *www.eriecanal.org/UnionCollege/175th-add.html*

Watt Steam Engine James Watt's steam engine helped power the Industrial Revolution. To view photos and a sketch of his engines, go to *www.egr.msu.edu/~lira/supp/steam/wattengine.htm*

RESOURCES

Books

Brezina, Corona. *The Industrial Revolution in America: A Primary Source History of America's Transformation into an Industrial Society*. New York: Rosen, 2005.

Hamen, Susan E. *Industrial Revolution*. Vero Beach, FL: Rourke Publishing, 2010.

Hillstrom, Kevin. *The Industrial Revolution*. Detroit: Lucent Books, 2009.

McNeese, Tim. *The Erie Canal: Linking the Great Lakes*. New York: Chelsea House, 2009.

Orr, Tamra B. *The Steam Engine*. New York: Franklin Watts, 2005.

Robinson Masters, Nancy. *The Cotton Gin*. New York: Franklin Watts, 2006.

Shea, Kitty. *Industrial America*. Minneapolis: Compass Point Books, 2005.

Wyatt, Lee T., III. *The Industrial Revolution*. Westport, CT: Greenwood Press, 2009.

Web Sites

Eastern Illinois University—Childhood Lost: Child Labor During the Industrial Revolution

www.eiu.edu/eiutps/childhood.php

Visit this site to learn about the lives of children who worked in factories and the people who tried to help them.

The Erie Canal

www.eriecanal.org

Check out this site for detailed information about the construction and history of the Erie Canal, along with many pictures and maps.

GLOSSARY

consumer (kuhn-SOO-mur) someone who buys and uses products and services

federal (FED-ur-uhl) referring to a system of government that balances power between states and the national government, or another name for the national government

innovations (in-uh-VAY-shuhnz) new ideas or inventions

loom (LOOM) a machine for weaving threads or yarn to produce cloth

mechanized (MEH-kuh-nized) equipped with machinery that replaces human labor

navigable (NA-vuh-guh-bul) deep and wide enough for ships to pass

patented (PA-tunt-id) obtained a document giving an inventor the sole right to make or sell an invention

pollutants (puh-LOOT-uhnts) substances that contaminate the air or environment

shuttle (SHUHT-uhl) an instrument used in weaving to carry the thread back and forth

strike (STRIKE) when workers refuse to work in an attempt to make their employers meet their demands

textile (TEK-stile) a fabric or cloth that has been woven or knitted

threshing (THRESH-ing) separating the seed from a plant

transcontinental (trans-kon-tuh-NEN-tuhl) crossing a continent

INDEX

Page numbers in *italics* indicate illustrations.

ABOUT THE AUTHOR

Melissa McDaniel Melissa McDaniel is a writer and editor originally from Portland, Oregon. She has a bachelor's degree in history, with an emphasis on early America, and a master's degree in library science. McDaniel has written books for young people on subjects ranging from Ellis Island to Isaac Newton to life on the deep-sea floor. She lives in New York City with her husband, daughter, dog, and frog.